MY CURSIVE HANDWRITING WORKBOOK

Learn to Write Cursive from A to Z

Crystal Radke

Illustrations by Amir Abou Roumie

Scan the QR code for bonus
cursive alphabet practice pages.

callisto
publishing
an imprint of Sourcebooks

Copyright © 2024 by Callisto Publishing LLC
Cover and internal design © 2024 by Callisto Publishing LLC
Illustrations © Amir Abou Roumie
Art Director: Jami Spittler and Lisa Schreiber
Art Producer: Stacey Stambaugh
Editor: Jeanann Pannasch
Production Editor: Matthew Burnett
Production Manager: Riley Hoffman

Callisto Kids and the colophon are registered trademarks of Callisto Publishing LLC

Published by Callisto Publishing LLC C/O Sourcebooks LLC
P.O. Box 4410, Naperville, Illinois 60567-4410
(630) 961-3900
callistopublishing.com

This product conforms to all applicable CPSC and CPSIA standards.

Source of Production: PA Hutchison
Date of Production: April 2024
Run Number: 5039647

Printed and bound in the United States of America.
PAH 10 9 8 7 6 5 4 3 2 1

The *Write* Start

Welcome to this workbook! Did you know that we use a different part of our brain when we write in cursive compared to when we print or type? By writing in cursive, you are improving important thinking skills and language skills and working your memory.

As you progress through the book, make sure to read through the instructions in each section. Be sure you go in order, too. The exercises are specially organized to help you be successful. You might find it helpful to tilt the book as you write; angle it a little to the right if you are right-handed and left if you are left-handed.

You will start by learning how to form each letter of the alphabet. Each exercise includes a demonstration of the practice letter in a sentence—in uppercase or lowercase—to reflect the example on each page. Then you will learn how to connect some common two- and three-letter combinations. Finally, you'll form words and write full sentences.

This cursive writing book will teach you more than just how to write in cursive. It will also help remind you how awesome you are. The sentences aren't just to practice writing; they are all statements about *you*! When you read the emphasized words that go along with each letter, proudly believe that they are true for your life.

You'll be stimulating your brain, feeling empowered, and learning how to write in cursive. Wow! You are going to love this book.

Happy writing.

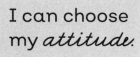
Trace and write the cursive letter.

4

Trace and write the cursive letter.

Every day offers a
new *Adventure.*

Trace and write the cursive letter.

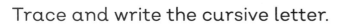

Trace and write the cursive letter.

7

Trace and write the cursive letter.

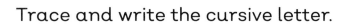

Today is a
new *chance.*

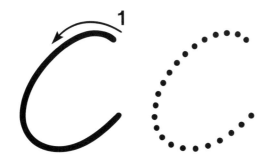

Trace and write the cursive letter.

Trace and write the cursive letter.

I can *dance* to the beat of my own *drum*.

Trace and write the cursive letter.

Don't be afraid
to Dream big.

Trace and write the cursive letter.

Trace and write the cursive letter.

I am *Enough.*

Trace and write the cursive letter.

I give myself permission to have *fun*.

Trace and write the cursive letter.

Trace and write the cursive letter.

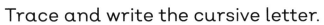

I choose to focus on the *good.*

Mistakes help me *Grow*.

Trace and write the cursive letter.

Trace and write the cursive letter.

Trace and write the cursive letter.

Trace and write the cursive letter.

Trace and write the cursive letter.

I can *Inspire* others with my words and actions.

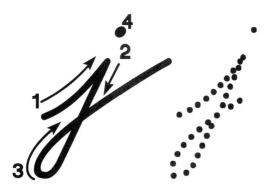

Trace and write the cursive letter.

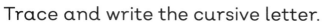

I deserve *Joy.*

Trace and write the cursive letter.

Trace and write the cursive letter.

If you never try, you'll never *know*.

I plant *Kindness* wherever I go.

Trace and write the cursive letter.

Trace and write the cursive letter.

26

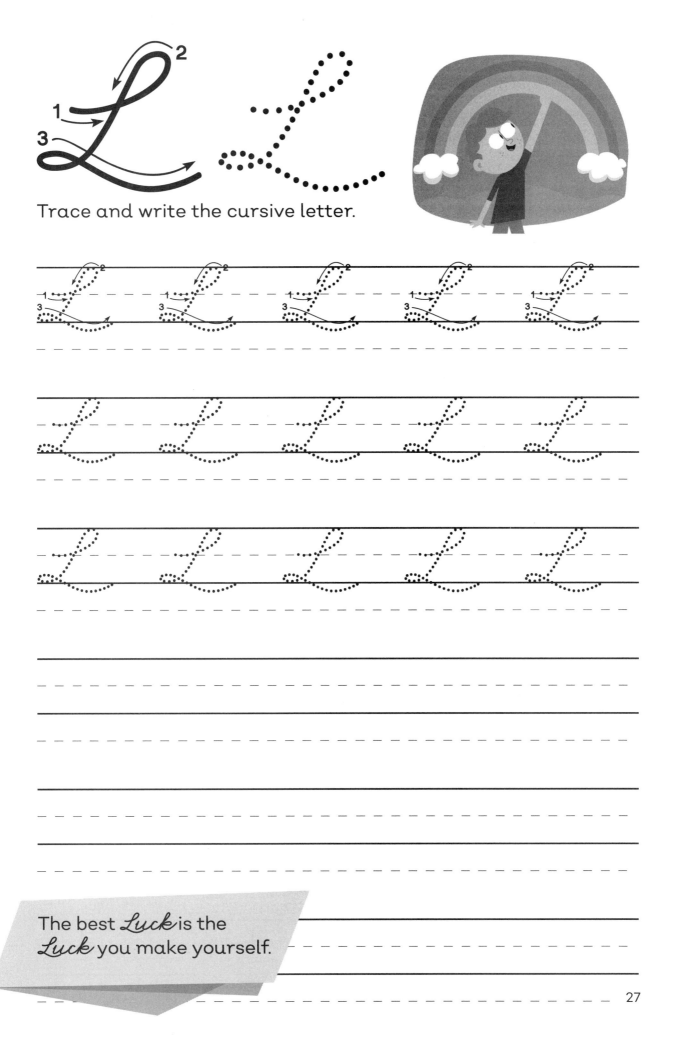

Trace and write the cursive letter.

The best *Luck* is the
Luck you make yourself.

$\mathcal{M}$ $\mathcal{M}$

Trace and write the cursive letter.

$\mathcal{M}$ $\mathcal{M}$ $\mathcal{M}$ $\mathcal{M}$ $\mathcal{M}$ $\mathcal{M}$

m m m m m m m

m m m m m m m

Trace and write the cursive letter.

I believe in *Myself.*

29

Trace and write the cursive letter.

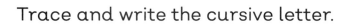

I *never* give up!

We *Need* each other.

Trace and write the cursive letter.

Trace and write the cursive letter.

There is *only one* you.

Trace and write the cursive letter.

Trace and write the cursive letter.

Trace and write the cursive letter.

Difficult *Paths* lead to sweet *Places.*

Trace and write the cursive letter.

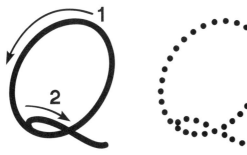

Trace and write the cursive letter.

Even when I'm *Quiet,* my words have power.

Trace and write the cursive letter.

You can't have a *rainbow* without a little *rain.*

Trace and write the cursive letter.

Trace and write the cursive letter.

I am *stronger* than peer pressure.

Trace and write the cursive letter.

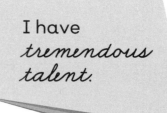

I have *tremendous talent.*

Trace and write the cursive letter.

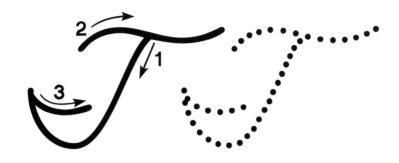

Trace and write the cursive letter.

I don't just survive, I *Thrive*.

Trace and write the cursive letter.

Trace and write the cursive letter.

I am *Unstoppable*
and will never give *Up.*

Trace and write the cursive letter.

Trace and write the cursive letter.

Trace and write the cursive letter.

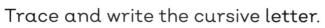

Every now and then, it's fun to *walk* on the *wild* side.

Trace and write the cursive letter.

Trace and write the cursive letter.

Trace and write the cursive letter.

Trace and write the cursive letter.

52

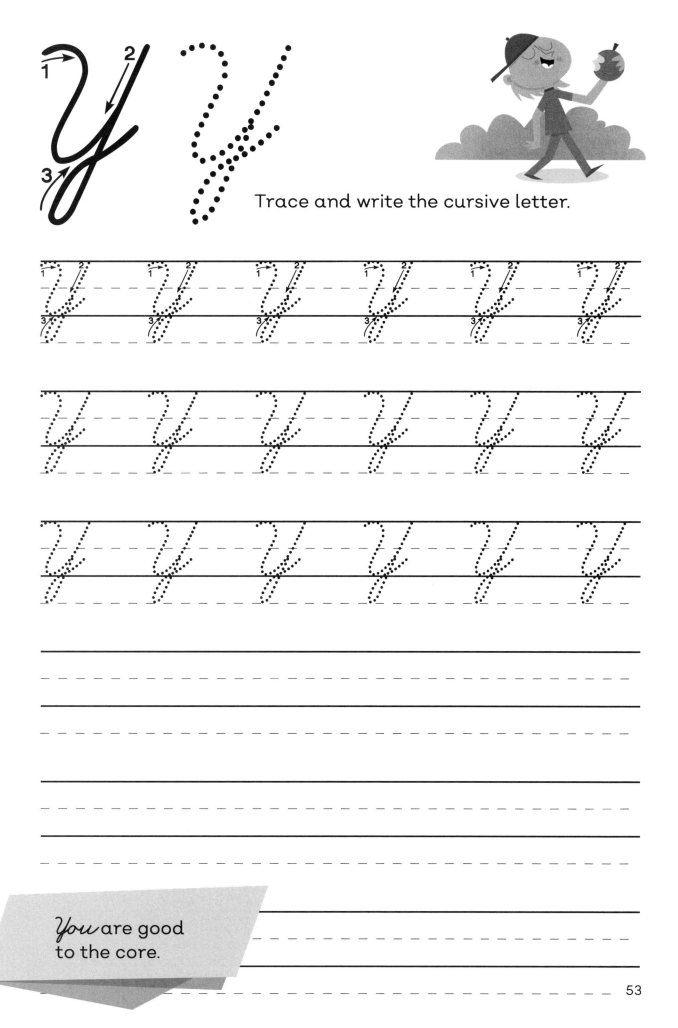

Trace and write the cursive letter.

You are good
to the core.

Trace and write the cursive letter.

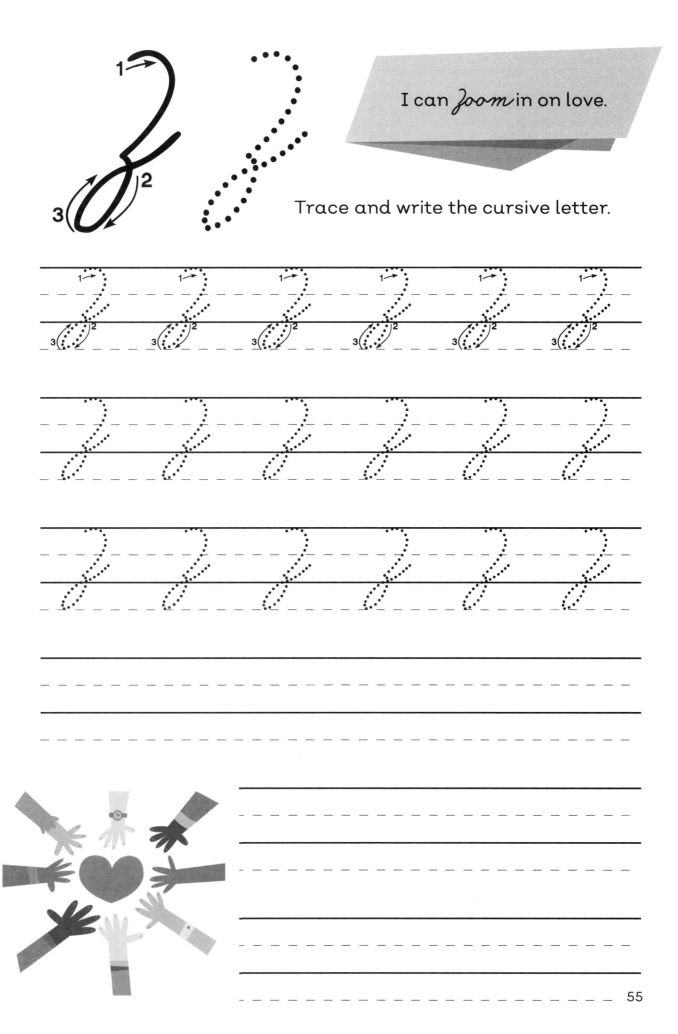

I can *zoom* in on love.

Trace and write the cursive letter.

Trace and write connecting cursive letters.

_ai ai_

_Br Br_

_ch ch_

_Ou Ou_

_el el_

_Fl Fl_

Trace and write connecting cursive letters.

Trace and write connecting cursive letters.

mp mp

na na

oe oe

Pr Pr

qu qu

Ri Ri

Trace and write connecting cursive letters.

Trace and write connecting cursive letters.

Trace and write fun words in cursive.

Awesomeness

Brilliant

Caring

Trace and write fun words in cursive.

devoted

Excited

funny

Trace and write fun words in cursive.

Grateful

happy

Inspiring

Trace and write fun words in cursive.

joyful

Knowledgable

loving

Trace and write fun words in cursive.

Motivating

mice

Outgoing

positive

Quick

island

Trace and write fun words in cursive.

Smart

thoughtful

Useful

Trace and write fun words in cursive.

vibrant

Wonderful

genial

Trace and write fun words in cursive.

Yourself

just

Trace and write fun sentences in cursive.

My dreams can

come true.

Trace and write fun sentences in cursive.

Today is a

fresh start.

Trace and write fun sentences in cursive.

I can learn

new things.

Trace and write fun sentences in cursive.

I am worthy

of love.

Trace and write fun sentences in cursive.

I am a role model.

I am brilliant and brave.

Trace and write fun sentences in cursive.

I can do hard things.

Anyone can

make a

difference.

Trace and write fun sentences in cursive.

Today is a
great day to try
something new.

Trace and write fun sentences in cursive.

Every swimmer

was once a

beginner.

Trace and write fun sentences in cursive.

The time is now

to be who I

want to be.

Trace and write fun sentences in cursive.

I do not have

to be perfect to

be amazing.

Trace and write fun sentences in cursive.

Start each day

with a grateful

heart.

Trace and write in cursive. Finish the sentence and sign your name.

I am awsome

because

Trace and write in cursive. Finish the sentence and sign your name.

I am proud of

myself for

Trace and write in cursive. Finish the sentence and sign your name.

I am happy

when

Trace and write in cursive. Finish the sentence and sign your name.

My friends

inspire me to

Trace and write in cursive. Finish the sentence and sign your name.

I am excited

for

Trace and write in cursive. Finish the sentence and sign your name.

My favorite part

of being me is

Trace and write in cursive. Finish the sentence and sign your name.

I am grateful

for my family

because

Trace and write in cursive. Finish the sentence and sign your name.

I feel strong

when

Trace and write in cursive. Finish the sentence and sign your name.

The challenge

I face will help

me

Trace and write in cursive. Finish the sentence and sign your name.

My favorite

activities are

Trace and write in cursive. Finish the sentence and sign your name.

I have fun by

Trace and write in cursive. Finish the sentence and sign your name.

The best part of

growing up is